Edward Lear's
Scrapbook

Michaela Morgan

OXFORD
UNIVERSITY PRESS

OXFORD
UNIVERSITY PRESS

Great Clarendon Street, Oxford, OX2 6DP, United Kingdom

Oxford University Press is a department of the University of Oxford. It furthers the University's objective of excellence in research, scholarship, and education by publishing worldwide. Oxford is a registered trade mark of Oxford University Press in the UK and in certain other countries

British Library Cataloguing in Publication Data
Data available

ISBN: 978-0-19-830800-3

10 9 8 7 6 5 4 3

Paper used in the production of this book is a natural, recyclable product made from wood grown in sustainable forests. The manufacturing process conforms to the environmental regulations of the country of origin.

Printed in China by Leo Paper Products Ltd

Acknowledgements

Series Editor: Nikki Gamble
Illustrations by: Deborah Zemke
Cover photos: Shutterstock/Daniel Cozma; Shutterstock/A. Kaiser; Shutterstock/oriontrail; Shutterstock/extradeda; The Bodleiain Library, University of Oxford 2014; 2529e.2; Alamy/V&A Images

p2t: The National Portrait Gallery/McLean, Melhuish & Haes; **p2b**: The Bodleiain Library, University of Oxford 2014; 2529e.2; **p6** & **p7t**: Alamy/V&A Images; **p7b**: The Royal Archives/©HM Queen Elizabeth II 2012; **p8l**: Corbis/stapleton collection; **p8r**: Alamy/V&A Images; **p9l**: Shutterstock/A. Kaiser; **p9r**: The National Portrait Gallery /Edward Lear; **p10**: Wikipedia Commons (out of copyright); **p11**: Bridgeman Art Library/Edward Lear; **p12** & **p13**: The Bodleiain Library, University of Oxford 2014; 2529e.2; **p14t**: Shutterstock/A. Kaiser; **p14**: Alamy/V&A Images; **p15**: Topfoto/The Grainger Collection, New York; Background images: Shutterstock/ Daniel Cozma; Shutterstock/A. Kaiser; Shutterstock/oriontrail; Shutterstock/extradeda; Shutterstock/A. Kaiser.

Edward Lear was an artist and a poet. He lived from 1812 to 1888.

Edward Lear

The Owl and the Pussy-cat

Contents

DREAM 37399

When I Was Little

My name is Edward Lear. I was born in London, England, in 1812.

I had lots of brothers and sisters. I was one of the youngest.

My family didn't have enough money. When I was four years old, I was sent away from home. I went to live with my big sister, Ann.

Ann

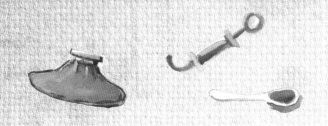

Ann looked after me. I needed a lot of looking after because I was ill so much.

I had sniffs and sneezes. I had coughs and wheezes. I had shivers and shakes and gloominess. I often felt sad.

Me!

My Paintings

I loved drawing. I started to make money from my art when I was 15 years old.

I liked to draw pictures of birds.

I **published** my first book in 1830, when I was 17 years old.

It was filled with pictures of parrots.

MACROCERCUS ARARAUNA.
Blue & Yellow Maccaw
¾ Nat. size

Later, I even gave
drawing lessons to
Queen Victoria.

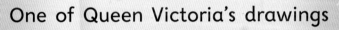
One of Queen Victoria's drawings

My Travels

I wanted to find out more about birds and different places.

So I went travelling.

lovely

very hot

sandy

R LONDON 3739 No. 43

The Crimson Bird.

The Light=Green Bird.

Post Card

for correspondence   for address only

domestic
one pence
foreign
three pence

I made up funny
poems and pictures
and put them in
my letters. My
friends liked them!

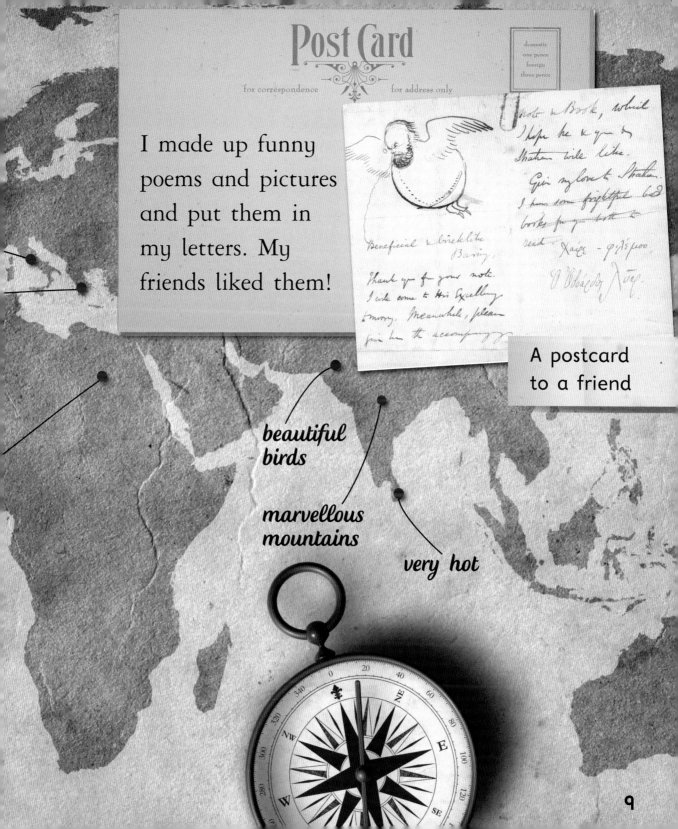

A postcard
to a friend

beautiful
birds

marvellous
mountains

very hot

My Poems

In 1846, I published my first book of poems. It was called *A Book of Nonsense*.

There were 72 poems in it!

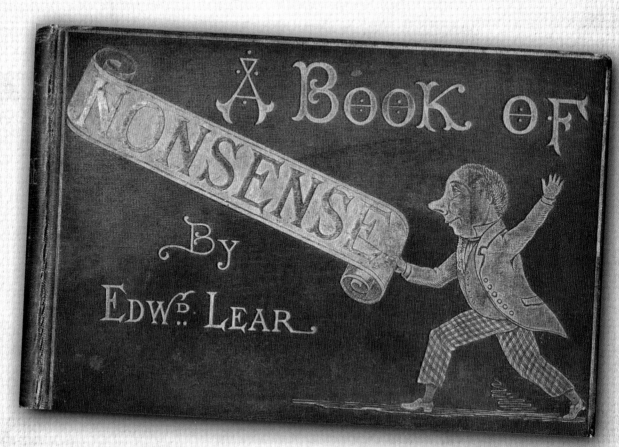

I wrote many short, funny poems. I called them 'nonsenses'. Other people called them **limericks**. Here's one:

> There was an Old Man with a beard,
> Who said, "It is just as I feared!
> Two Owls and a Hen,
> Four Larks and a Wren,
> Have all built their nests in my beard!"

There was an Old Man with a beard, who said, "It is just as I feared!—
Two Owls and a Hen, four Larks and a Wren,
Have all built their nests in my beard!"

My Characters

The Owl and
the Pussy-cat

When I was working, I dreamed a bit ...
I doodled a bit ... I let my mind wander.
I made up strange characters and gave them
wonderful names – like Jumblies and Pobble
and Dong. Then I sent them on adventures.

the Jumblies

the Pobble

the Dong

I had fun drawing and writing. I worked hard so that I could earn money to buy food. My favourite things to eat were bread and cheese.

When I Was Old

When I was old, I wanted to live in the sun. I moved to Italy with my cat, Foss.

Foss grew old and one day, she died. It was sad but she had lived a good life. I gave her a big **funeral**.

Edward Lear died in January 1888.

People still enjoy his books and poems today.
Try reading *The Owl and the Pussy-cat*, his
most famous poem.

The Owl and the Pussy-cat went to sea
In a beautiful pea-green boat,
They took some honey, and plenty of money
Wrapped up in a five pound note.

Glossary

funeral: a ceremony for someone who has died

limericks: funny poems with five lines

published: when a book is printed and ready for everyone to read

Queen Victoria: the British queen from 1837 to 1901

Some of Edward Lear's poems that you might like:

- *The Dong with the Luminous Nose*

- *The Jumblies*

- *The Owl and the Pussy-cat*

- *The Quangle Wangle's Hat*

- *The Pobble Who Has No Toes*